My Daily Actions, or The Meteorites

POETS OUT LOUD

Elisabeth Frost, *series editor*

My Daily Actions, or
The Meteorites

S. Brook Corfman

Fordham University Press New York 2020

Contents

All things possible do happen, only
what happens is possible

—FRANZ KAFKA

Matter is desperate

—ETEL ADNAN

Foreword *Cathy Park Hong*

S. Brook Corfman's *My Daily Actions, or The Meteorites* is an exquisitely crafted account of a vanishing world. Reminiscent of Lyn Hejinian's *My Life* for our anthropocene era, Corfman writes mesmerizing sentences that can stand on their own, like messages in a bottle washed up from our ever expanding sea. Consider this line: "I understand repression as an absence still filling the lungs with water." Or the following line: "I believe again in astrology because it seems as arbitrary as gender." Corfman infuses much tenderness and felt wisdom and imagination in each of these seeming truisms.

The meteor, hurtling toward Earth, is a speculative fantasy of our impending extinction, but it is also a metaphor of the self's interior (note the intended rhyme) as they consider "disowning" the gender they were born with while cultivating another gender into "being." The collection works as a conceit of diary entries—interspersed with a section of austere monostix lyric poems—but there is nothing hasty or random in Corfman's prose poems, which all seem considered with such painstaking care that I want to read them again and again. *My Daily Actions, or The Meteorites* tracks our existential dread with both worldly and solitary astonishment.

My Daily Actions, or The Meteorites

Premonition

In the field hands rise like wildflowers.

Each nail painted a bright color—teal, sunflower, tangerine, lapis.

From your vessel, dip the paddle to the dirt.

It moves as water, a reversed river.

A single door, ornate, leads only to the rest of the meadow.

When I am alone, I sometimes stand like the women of those worlds which are my own sacred texts.

I hold a scepter shaped like a key, turn from the Torah toward a magical girl.

A beautiful form appears with a warning: the valley will burn, or the sky will firm as weight.

These are not inevitable, but I react to specific demands.

For example, let time move forward.

Never go through the door.

So, I wait and watch what moves in the meadow.

Each step toward or away from the door becomes impossibly detailed.

Meteor

If I focus on the window, the trees move me south. Birch, acacia, willow, oak, these are not their names. One question is about how much can be willed into the world, whether this is a form of activism or a deadly distraction. Similarly, an electronic bird gathers data about rainforest animals far from my own, as the study population slowly diminishes. That is, I recently imagined living for 900 years. So much cruelty. When even ten years ago I could barely imagine crossing twenty. Autocorrect: bare image. I create in my mind each next square, but it is so much effort. The glass darkens with it. Dog using his tail as a brush erasing the path. That's wonderland, that's right now. I wished to become a starfish collecting human hair softly in the ocean, beautiful in my slow accumulation of toxins. Take them in, take them in, they lull me irregularly to sleep.

It is as if a meteor is imminent. It is as if to walk out of a house in a pair of heels would make me someone's hero and also get me killed. It is as if this is not statistically unlikely, for me. It is as if, what was the word the therapist used, my sense of self was annihilated as a child. As if I do not hold tension but work very hard to be tired or tense from other activities. As if I ever captured a spider instead of killing it. Sometimes the window slips down. It has nothing to do with circadian rhythm. It is as if I stayed up all night because I could pretend no one would call upon me. Sometimes I feel betrayed by the early morning birds, whatever kind live in Western Pennsylvania. I wanted everything to be asleep and to leave me alone, to stop talking to each other in ways I could not understand, and then I took to myself with such precise penance.

I am surprised by my vision of disaster. I always thought I would prefer water. Fountain of youth overflowing until I drown. Swimming, a skill I do have, until I am filled with acid and sink, a stone. Gabby wrote how easy it was to become a stone and it is not the same for me. I wish I could forget. And should I die tomorrow. I am instead a burning sphere moving through space. That is, I am a sphere moving through space and burn only when I get close to another mass. In a Sailor Moon movie, which I own on VHS although I don't myself own a VCR player, silver rays give way to a pink bubble that converts the meteor, comfortably holding six, into a space ship. We can all breathe. Even if Tuxedo Mask kissed me back to life, all Endymion, I think I would stay dead and be grateful to have gone out that way.

Let me say this one thing, that the meteor is a woman of varying biologies and the crocuses are rising up. In only three words I can convey a schism: x, y, z. Insert here for pleasure. The increasing question of if anything is scientific: we have sensations unreliably programmed. The wall's texture is uncomfortable. That is, the fan moves air into and out of a white room, where otherwise it stultifies.

It's hot in here. Thrown rock at a head and rising water. Or sewage. A euphemism for shit in your lake. Was it true all the pipes in the bathroom went to the same place, as the cartoon about anal sex suggested? I'd always thought they held us differently. Still, an ice shelf will break off tomorrow. The day after tomorrow will cut your leg on a rusty car door. A sensibility for perseverance I clearly lack.

I hold the dysphoria in a clean line. Rich green triangle. In high school I made drawings of silhouettes, big paintings of blue rings locked in chains. It seems so obvious, now, what they knew before I did. This is not divorceable from my body behind them, and I am working to make it clear: every line has been drawn, every work the result of a moving hand. Kerry said, to the room, "A complex notion of causality does not estrange us from responsibility." I would have said absolve but it was too perfect to change. Still, I am attached to the category of human. I see it in the clay they perform into a sculpture. I read research on the pineal gland, how hormones are probably to blame. I mean for everything. I am an identical twin and yet what is similar about us. The brushfire we put out every day for two years until the effort of it fells the trees inside. Punctuation, punctuation, punctuation, punctuation, estrangement.

In lieu of screaming a sound internal. Wroar. Whirring. Then, not. Then, not. Ritual of release or mourning. A carefully drawn line can not only demarcate, but create. A crowd on one side of the page. Interlocked like lace. I couldn't have imagined I would begin drawing again, but I did. Randomness allowed, as a belief that has been building. Or perhaps abstraction, that it is so personal. "If you feel you are, you are" "an abstraction with a nice attachment." And so I move through the world having disowned what I worked so hard to attain, this man, although I never could convince anyone I was cruel. A masculinity participated in. A hot tub just sitting there, people in, people out.

I love all the songs other people hate. The television conveys beauty to me like a receptacle. When fish die they float to the top of the tank, turn colors as they're cooked. Mostly. A stenciled T-shirt changes colors too, like a lantern at the prow. The mermaid saw it and was captured in wood. Perhaps I mean that literally. Speak the location and see who comes running: from the flat world, each family breaks apart when pushed. Like glass, millions of pressure points so as to reduce injury. Instead I'm cut millions of times as my mother walks through an invisible door. Each shard a bleedingheart flower. No, the flower, how it opens at dusk for a bright stone.

Walking through my apartment I heard someone say "en guard!" like they were in my ear. Perhaps it was a kind of hallucination. When I wandered to the coffee shop there were no seats and everyone looked up at me as I entered.

It's true, our living room is extremely warm and has large windows. Once I had a vision and sat upon the table. My failure reminded me of the gap between my skills as the audience of art and as an aerator. I mean artist. A spider crawled slowly up a single strand of web in front of my face, and I couldn't help but wonder: did he come from my hair? What else is there to hang on to?

It's worth saying, too, that I am obsessed with the distraction of the meteor I can hold: I am listening to my shoulder blades rub together, a sound of my interior I am pretty sure I can actually hear. An internet quiz tells me I strive to be both "austere" and "exquisitely composed." Like that quiz I believe again in astrology because it seems as arbitrary as gender. Sailor Moon's strong emotions become a laser, however much we try to pretend it's benevolent. At first no one believes I am a Pisces, but then they read the poems.

The shadow of a hair as it grows longer unfurls into the leg of a preying mantis. No one sleeps and we are already dead. We are accepting this, or I am trying to do so without giving up. If the prism scatters, still we hold each color together until we reach a new surface. There are no excuses. A book I read telegraphs the truth of an experience, or one truth, in a real kind of realism like perfumed hair. A speculative moth under the moon. A speculative tulip bulb which grows into other kinds of bulbs: Edison's, scientists. Multi-purpose latex has been engineered to grant you vision in the dark, even if you did not have vision in the light. I am happy for this vision of a life but wish for a transformation instead. I have never read a book that mirrored my gender and like books anyway: is it unnecessary, then, or is there an absence that, if filled, would flood? Again, I understand calm as an absence. I understand repression as an absence still filling the lungs with water.

Along with the backing track, in which a marble sphere thuds, the question arises: do I not want children? It seems the cloud has risen among us into a trajectory. There is no more sand to be found. I feel eternally pubescent as I associate my gender into being. It turns out, I may be becoming older. Eternal gerund. The paleozoolithic leaf that fans me quietly can as easily be held by my own hands as a little girl's. The blinds unfurl as sheaves of water down a matrilineal line.

The tv filters from the other room: are private feelings really public? A closed question. The way that therapists say things you'd exactly expect them to say, and they become profound: just because everyone dies doesn't mean you must outrun their death. Social pressures affect me even when I am alone. I realize there's a window open even though the air conditioner is on, but it's cool in my bed so I don't get up to close it. I lay motionless for several hours but do not sleep. Remember my friend who found it easy to become a stone? We are lying here, spraying ourselves down, praying desperately to slide sideways to the river.

I have not become a lion, a wolf, not even a lizard. I have been ineffective. I wanted to be a starfish, hurtling through a void. All that's left is detritus fused together like the island of trash in the Pacific. Like that island, these too retain importance, I just can't figure out how to tell you. Importance can take us in many directions. What if I said I came from the future and the world had ended, and it was important to write down how your mind collided with itself? What if I said I greyed up below the surface, woke only to see the fire cross the firebreak? I am not describing my day well, but I'm not trying to escape it either.

Bioaerosols diffuse in the air as a wall. It all heads toward me. I dream the ocean gives chase, and it does. The heat. I am trying to explain that I am as afraid as the pale girl screaming, every sound's small death. Where I put my hand, below my skin, I feel a pistachio shell. I wanted only to be possessed so I could truthfully say I was never close to anyone. I wanted to die but only in certain ways. This swinging rope, heavy with electricity, it wasn't on the list. The lichen turns right at the corner and covers the fountain. The petals turn left. Something is at the bottom, has filled without air.

The sky lights up as we turn the corner to a wedding. I'm alone, yes, but I'm happy for them. It's a town with only one late night bar, and the one time we went they blamed the victim. An army commercial makes me think about how I still somehow want the individuals in them to arbitrarily "succeed" (at what? not the war) even though I think the military should be abolished. A circle drawn in brass around an aspiration, or the deed to a house. Not the object itself. There's a body and a body and a body and a feeling and they're all different from each other. I sometimes imagine a god I don't ever want to meet. Of spun planets and a broken hourglass. We do not yet know how I feel.

It is an appropriate time to return to the impending ecological disaster, its dread. A microwave being constructed slowly around me. There are other dreads, and they are related—people I love could be shot at any moment, "ancient grains" are leached from the communities that they could feed—so I am turning to an interval between concrete and anxiety. I cannot imagine a death star. It is helpful to change one's habits to address a root cause, although one could also fend off any perennial bulb at its encounter every time. It feels important to say we no longer "hang up" most phones, even landlines, in the literal sense. A mysterious underneath spatially organized. I'm not lost, exactly, but I wouldn't know how to get there again if you asked me to show you.

Today it was hot and then suddenly I wasn't wearing enough clothing. I want to wear a romper. Do you feel unsupported? There is a line: idealism or structures. I'm trying to do everything I've ever done in a dream in real life. Creating installation art saying "FAILURE" in different neons—that was Gabby's dream, and I'm proud of it. Other dreams: fighting with my boyfriend, witch hunting, getting lost in a water park, dying, cutting off the head of my middle school gym teacher. I learned most of what I know about embodiment from women, and the rest from the internet. Only then did I read the theory. Three book covers: teardrops, tears, and a collage. A flag a prison a bar code up against a dead woman or a still photograph. When I took a selfie I learned I had a pimple I hadn't felt. When I took a selfie there was a man in the picture I hadn't seen before. If this were Criminal Minds, I'd be next to die.

Have you forgotten about my body, its particulars. The implication here is that I did, somehow, successfully. And then I didn't sleep well and my eyes felt more particular while everything else blurred. The window clicks shut. I do this as a routine. When we don't lock it, the top falls down like a blouse and spiders get in that easily. I feel little remorse but wonder. I still could not take it lightly that people made love without me, I misremember that quote. A hanger falls from the chandelier like a raven. Sulfur. I turned my attitude up to confuse you and it worked. I am here and here is the sand I removed to make a space.

It is as if "tired" is no longer a response, a physicality that occurs as the result of something, but instead a pre-emptive (autocorrect: pre-emotive) mentality to being called upon. The theorists call this "being hailed." I call it receiving an email between three and nine pm. And then the phone rang in ten-minute intervals, and it was revealed the great fact that would fill the day: a woman died. A woman died and we cannot even agree she was a woman. A woman died in horrible ways and the statistics didn't change but I felt their failure more clearly. Only the boyfriend checked on me. I cannot tell if this is because only the boyfriend knows. It is hard to talk about. And yet I have filled a notebook.

Apparent Corona

—*Myung Mi Kim*

First name last name harm.

First name last name death.

Flowers are beautiful.

This is heavy.

Someone else will drink the wine.

First name last name prize.

Snow falls as rain.

Mucus accumulates.

A plan one year in advance.

Feeling of belonging to the imminent past.

Sphere blue with futility.

Face ruptures.

Stress thump.

Stress thump.

Strange fullness.

The heat turns on.

White footpath.

Diamond circle.

Brain and brain and skull.

Vanishing steps.

There is no obvious correlation to the poem.

Bloomed skin, red rash.

Anallergic.

Illicit profusion.

Each chapped lip takes in dust.

I have to emerge into the world.

Small series of replacements.

Quotidian effect of pain.

I wake up tired.

The failure lain down to sleep.

I throw what little energy I have left at the wall.

The scars in continual rupture.

Open mouth.

Lip & whitehead.

The human skin regenerating cleanly.

(The scar erodes.)

How is it a virus is not contagious.

Little bloom.

Little archipelago under the skin.

I google thrush, I google anxious death.

I seem to be truly changing.

It is not twilight.

Other names are fear or grief.

To move on and through a feeling, the feeling must be honored.

Some encounters could have been avoided.

A scream.

The screen shakes.

I am not crying.

I want this blurred hour to continue.

New room.

I felt as if a stranger walked through the wall.

The heart rate settles.

The heart rate rises.

A time span holds sadness.

A shape like a holster.

COLD METEOR

The eye is greedy, a faint glow at the edge of a bed. It is rising like the night sky. It cannot cease. When I removed my mask nothing looked like I'd been to the club. When I removed my mask I knew time was up, at least for me. Impossible venture until it happens. The balloon inflates into a meteor; California slides partially into the ocean. I wished for overlapping circles as representations of the parts of my life. I wished for an avatar to move through the world looking however I wished it to. It may have been granted, in some small part. It fell upon him. Will fall. I blamed my curtains for my insomnia, but then the fan on the ceiling shook itself loose, popped the window open and rain flooded in. A daffodil I seem to have dropped on my way home. How intensity fades or collects on a spinning blade.

A long leg and a purse walk into a room. There is no joke. The record skips as if I had a record. I, I, I, I, uh oh. We film the motion four times. If we can do things three times we can do them seven. The dj forgot my friend was performing and this was the third time in a month someone had accidentally forgotten a black friend. I insert and remove air quotes as text, in an attempt to mark the deeply specific yet also abstracted racism. The record skips to an Elvis ballad, not to Rosetta Tharpe. We're all at a party. Naomi is frantic and the drinks are strong. Anxiety cracks my skull. A horse comes straight for me. Insect wings are my new obsession.

I was in an orchard. My hair grew behind me like the tail of some fast sphere. A worst fear: cauliflower ear. I can't hear about the vegetable without thinking of the football players. The only feeling to which I have a corresponding acute physical sensation is disgust, the shudder of cotton mouth it tries to disperse. Or this fear of pain and that it might happen to me. Why is it a yelled name from a stranger is hurtful? Consider annihilation in small doses, how it can be accomplished by anyone. I'm still afraid of the bakery cashier, and it's been five years. Say, you don't look pink. Say, pink is not the color. It's difficult to detach pink from inherent value. See the heat-soaked cobblestones. Even at night, there's no relief. Pink floods the inside of the eyelid.

But also, it was in the way we responded to things, how some jokes seemed to "catch" on a face, pull it toward or away from an utterance. By "we" of course I mostly mean just me. Meanwhile Danielle writes "meanwhile, that tree outside can be sad if I think it so," and as I grew older I became more easily confused for or confirmed as comfortable. I wore a backward baseball cap for the first time, grew my hair but not an intentional beard. I pretended a certain kind of beauty had silver in it, and in a way it was. I lay in bed with a pink lion and a bodily mechanism that released a tear—something about my proprioceptive orientation, how my chest sacrificed itself for the sensations held only in my face.

A confession of my inadequacy: there is something I love I want to replicate but I fear I am succeeding. Circumscribed time balloons. As a car moves through it the fog condenses to rain. That is, the self in the thin statue at the entranceway, of bronzed copper. The sled as red metal in the snow. Again for hours along a highway, up against a truck, in brighter clouds and then encroaching frost. A feeling is different each time but that does not mean it is absent a form.

Struck with a stick a knowledge inside me shifts, clicks. Seen by a snake I become again. As if pulling kumquats, golden delicious, blackberries, taro root. Each empty of its sugar, of any juice. In time cataracts overtake every eye, not as punishment. I took a name—Lydia, Prudence, opposites—and whispered it in the ear of the wind.

I am trying not to research anything consciously, but this is also an excuse. Baby animals filter through. Dana: "the earth is in pain and we can feel it." I worry we are talking about the impending ecological disaster instead of the current one. I worry we are talking about the impending ecological disaster instead of [   ]. Hello? The hello delay; I don't know to what this refers. It is perhaps a technological concept that is also a poem. I speak "microphone" and one appears. I tell myself I still have "muscle memory" for the instruments of my youth. This time, a glass rose. In one scholarly field, there's a mantra—the more produced, the fewer individual examples that survive. Another mantra, of my grandmother's: what's very expensive should not bear a brand. But also, such a vacancy might indicate the opposite. An opening.

When I called my friend I wanted to say don't you love me the best. When I called my twin I waited for him to speak. I started collaging again. I started pasteling again. I put the pencil down and smudged it with my fingers. The rain came in through the open window. I wanted the Catholic gesture of prayer, the comfort of ceremony, but it seems my people only sit, stand, or sway.

I wondered how the world would end, am convinced again it will be water as my frozen skull becomes attuned to a certain crackle. Seeping feeling into the feet. Intertwined in ivy and beholden to a woman in a valley. The rain fell harder as the road rose; to be sure, I was afraid. There's a kind of suspension in a car on a highway, so that to stop feels a great affront. No space travel, just different materials. We're becoming better actors, so we're beholden to redo everything we did before with our more efficient or precise technology. When I went to the bottom of the lake I found a door there, and it opened into a temple that rose into the sky.

. . . I fear I've pushed too far. I tumbled over my own muscle, it seized up, strained as the words associate. Is it too intentional? Sure, the dragonfly wing reflects the puddle back. I feel it is important but distrust my own impressions, how I value the silk flash over the metal. The lower abdominals, the forehead: here gather the propulsive forces. A dandelion whitening and dispersing. Let it be softer than I imagine.

Each exhibit was a different environment, even a branched sky, getting warmer. Three horses halt at a flash of lightning three siblings cannot feel. I do not press the button but expect the effect of it anyway. A horizontal line, and now it vanishes. I walk into a landscape, and suddenly there is a narrative like a cherry tree. There is a Philips head orchard, and everything grows. Your shadow joins me, a prismatic color. Can you point me can you point me can you point me can you point.

I cannot decide if I am also a new object. I do not think of myself as having good vision because I wear glasses; there is sensation in the eyes of irritation. And hunger. Is this an automatic process, how a dryer sheet collects each sultry mote to itself? Is this an unrestful mind sprawled on the ceiling of a kaleidoscopic home? There was nothing sexual there, sprawled on my back in the sun, not even when I encountered others' anxieties, naked. Yes madame therapist, I have not been very kind. Declared like the unused air that gathers in the backyard. Our three years are almost up, another of those irate red deadlines I've internalized. In the tea leaves a conflict arises. An end that draws near is no more than a horizon I stave off with a long paddle into the pond.

The steeping tea marks the feeling of waiting. I chose oolong, this time, and unlike other times the source is withheld. When heated, a woman does not recognize the leaves she previously disseminated. I too do not look closely at the shapes I contain, only the paths I send outward. I am a bad imitator and yet this is a good imitation, which is to say a bad paragraph. In what ways can a duplicate be as interesting as the original, if it claims to be different as a second steep, the small remnants of a seed at the bottom of a glass container.

There's a lens in my eye, and in one film an extra lens tipped off an assassin. At this point almost anything could be a fairy tale. The robot and the alien escape to elaborate asteroid rings. Photos of the planets do not reveal them. The streaked sky means it's been well used since I was a child. I used to sit at the edge of the lake as waves came in and try to predict precisely the path they would leave on the sand, their exact contour. I almost said it was more interesting than lines, but I'm interested in those too, how I could never achieve the precision my high school art teacher wanted from me. I've embraced it like an elegant glove, smudged with the ink from the drawing.

W stands for whitewater, as in how what was once clear is named. The invention of butter for many purposes, not all of them demure. If I tell you I read the tarot, and in it I saw a rock hurtling through space, propelled by an initial force. If the brontosaurus, like today's elephant, mourned. Even for other species' dead, better than us. Thinks we're cute, too, in the same part of the brain. An altered evolution. Like a cuffed rose. I laid down in the bed and didn't rise for several hours. I wore an emerald dress. It had a low back. The shape of a feathered wing as a knife coming together in the library. Then, inexplicably, a slow film and a blue one.

Can I tell you when I'm frustrated I sometimes hurt myself? Just lightly, a repeated pressure on my calf. A bluing. This is an improvement. This is the energy born forward from an anxiety, a small bee that, without belief, has entered, lost. The thin line the door fills, it separates one wall from the other and I can feel the shifting sequoia when I pass through. I move away from food as if from fire. The air conditioner keeps me trapped. Each cardiovascular shape working more or less correctly, if with decreasing efficiency.

There is an exchange at work, of attention, of a smooth texture I am elided from for one like paper. Each lightning bug spills from behind the bookcase. Each cold shipwreck in my mind. The television I watch almost invariably moves around what it means to take a life, although often becomes truly philosophical only unwittingly. The formula holds a deeply charged red, a halo. Once a man charged at a man and failed, and later he tried a different tactic. A natural life contained in a tank, with the dolphin. Natural natural natural natural natural natural said until it feels like a sentence where each word is a different part of speech. A syllogism, or only if you already knew it as overpouring.

Do you know what it is to absence? How the moon curls away from itself into the blanket of sky? "Look what the exiles must do in order to gain citizenship, to return to the house." The calendar's pages fall all out of order and even the fruit supports the war. Israel invented the cherry tomato, so I stopped buying them, used my cutting board much more for each beefsteak red. The bridge in the photograph is made to look old, and it's not very arresting, but in black and white and zoomed in it participates in a contemporary aesthetic. That is, it somehow looks flat.

During the séance, I kept quiet. The ashes alongside the lilies on the water. Each shifting scrim. A force behind movement that lied about its whereabouts: it wasn't me. I try to remind you about the mask in my bedroom, venetian carnival hung on the wall, how it fell and shattered. It was loud and heavy. Again, again, the lava rock in space. I jumped down to break the spell. I was grateful for the tall fence I'd built around me. The small rabbit hopped right through.

On a scream a naked form flew. Feral feeling but no just cause. A search party wove its way into the loom. We clothed her, the voice. It was not clear what fabric would do, other than warm. Once I become aware of an alternative it is difficult to continue on. Do not say it, it's coming I know it but I'm hoping you won't. The fan fell from the window again. That's how she got out. I'm a speculative mind. You were below sea level. A meteor, too, hung in the sky, coming closer. When the impression of a dinosaur's skin was discovered in the sand, I briefly believed in science. It was so close to the illustrations I had seen. On the meteor everything happening here happens also. No, nothing's different. A comet is cold, like a mirror in the forest.

I traced myself in peppermint oil, for protection. During the storm, each room filled with water, a jar always brimming. An escape from daily pronouns. Outside a fan still swung, slow whooms, whoom, and then it stopped.

The deer as an omen, ghosts stopped silently in the city's road. Unconcerned. They amble off, but they have rattled me. I, the death wail of each passing car; I, a late-night but still somehow bright sky. When I looked through the window from outside I brought down a spider web. When I opened the door, I had my phone to my ear, still locked, to show whatever was coming from the other side that I was not alone.

Premonition

I put on a coat made of paper where fear lines each side. To restore old books, the paper can be split in half

and reattached with a new archival center, to preserve it. I don't know what can be done with circuits and wires, but imagine edges meeting just beyond my finger. I painted my nails. That's why I chose this nexus. This doesn't mean anything as a theory of gender. I am training my left hand to be as adept as my right. I cannot decide if I am larger than my skin. The most expensive thing I ever touched was a book and somehow I was not afraid I would ruin it. As soon as I say,

no one has mentioned this color,

a woman comments on it. It makes me miss my friend, the geologist, whose favorite color is teal. Is it clear to you that "as soon" is actually indicative of a twenty-four-hour period, give or take a few hours? That the woman holds a staff shaped like a key and neither of us knows what kind of lock such a key opens?

The poet is in my ear, take notes, take notes, notes, notes, yes, notes.

As soon as I got back from the sequoias I put the smoky quartz in a box and the polish back on my fingers. Metallic sheen. I prayed at each ancient, each ossified corpse for a little more magic than I had in my life. When I held out my hand to the phone it did not fly across the room to me. The truth: I was disappointed. I am softening myself, and I cannot seem to distinguish this from becoming more like a child.

What if hysteria is a heuristic we can use to predict the future? Not Freud—picture Cassandra screaming unheeded or better yet a pop star "in hysterics after bombing"

as the internet tells me when I google "famous hysterics." As if these women had been recorded as individuals. These many-gendered women I feel so tender toward. When such a feeling is a bomb or a bullet crossing a gap, but what is the gap. I am afraid to go to the store alone. Each place I told a lie in I can see clearly, as I can see my father in the chair in the middle of the room

saying no I don't think it's a good idea

even though that chair was against the wall and I was on the stairs. My father must have said more than that. Yes, we were talking about nail polish and what was coming toward me, the man I was sure was going to launch himself

across the food court. The strange space where the fear might be justified but until it happens it seems there's nothing to be done. What color does the sky change when a "bad thing" is on the horizon, but it's not a storm or a tornado? That's the color of the interval between me and the man's possible violence. I regret not submerging myself in the very cold water called "mirror lake." I have always wanted to go through a mirror. I add this to my list. The list is longer than I remember it. There is one day that is cool and this reprieve makes every hot day after it seem impossible to stand. And then I saw a meteor

and then two, real ones, in the sky.

A meteor is only the action, the burning up. And the thing about them is, unless you're lucky, you only see them out of the corner of your eye. So you, like the meteor, are moving to a point of absence, just the night.

Notes

Wikipedia: "A meteorite is a solid piece of debris from an object, such as a comet, asteroid, or meteoroid, that originates in outer space and survives its passage through the Earth's atmosphere and impact with the Earth's surface or that of another planet." That "visible passage" is the meteor. These poems are the sleight-of-hand outcome of a compressed thought process, an associative—almost automatic—bodily output begun in 2017. An aggregation in the night.

They are haunted especially by Cassils' performances "Becoming an Image" (and the resultant sculpture) and "Tiresias," as well as Haegue Yang's art installations, including "Series of Vulnerable Arrangements—Domestics of Community" and the artist book *Wild Against Gravity.* Yang's installations are, to quote one essayist, "abstractions that have nice attachments."

I wrote "Apparent Corona" in February of 2018, borrowing its title from a phrase in Myung Mi Kim's 1999 book *Dura,* which also inspired the poem's form. Although both references are primarily to the "aura of plasma" around a star that is only sometimes evident, I have let the title stand in 2020 as record of that poem's own oblique premonition of the world it would come to inhabit.

In the closing premonition, "the poet" is CAConrad; "Danielle," earlier, is Danielle Dutton writing in *Sprawl.* Other quotes are from social media, or conversation.

Four works especially were also companions in form and pattern:

> *A poem is a meteor.* | Wallace Stevens c/o Elizabeth Willis in *Meteoric Flowers*
>
> *A comet with its ominous hair* | Marosa di Giorgio, trans. Adam Gianelli, in *Diadem*
>
> *the meteoric gaps into which things get absorbed* | Dawn Lundy Martin in *Discipline*
>
> *A throw of food and household goods from the roof / to all of us became a meteor shower across fixed stars* | Mei-Mei Berssenbrugge in *The Heat Bird*

Acknowledgments

These poems traveled uncertainly with me for a long time, and I'm so grateful for those who helped me understand how they lived: my impeccable stewards at Fordham, Elisabeth Frost and Richard Morrison; my loves, the geniuses Stephanie Cawley, Lucia LoTempio, Gabrielle Ralambo-Rajerison, and Steffan Triplett; exemplary artists Howardena Pindell, Yona Harvey, Brian Teare, Stacy Szymaszek, and Jessica Fisher; and, especially, Cathy Park Hong—the careful reader who crossed the strange space between possibility and event.

Gratitude to the editors of *Conjunctions, Indiana Review, The Offing, Omniverse,* the Poetry Project's *Recluse, Sycamore Review, Typo,* and *Territory,* who published selections from this work, sometimes with slightly different forms and titles. Excerpts from this work were honored as finalists for the *Iowa Review* Poetry Prize, the *Puerto del Sol* Poetry Prize, and the inaugural Chautauqua Janus Prize for Innovative Prose.

And to Anna, MC, & Jeff, who as DoubleCross Press published the section "Meteor" in a gorgeous letterpress edition as the chapbook, *Meteorites.*

S. Brook Corfman is the author of *Luxury, Blue Lace*, chosen by Richard Siken for the 2018 Autumn House Rising Writer Prize, and two chapbooks, including *The Anima: Four Closet Dramas* (Gauss PDF, 2019). Born and raised in Chicago, they now live in Pittsburgh.

POETS OUT LOUD
Prize Winners

José Felipe Alvergue

scenery: a lyric

S. Brook Corfman

My Daily Actions, or The Meteorites

Henk Rossouw

Xamissa

Julia Bouwsma

Midden

Gary Keenan

Rotary Devotion

Michael D. Snediker

The New York Editions

Gregory Mahrer

A Provisional Map of the Lost Continent

Nancy K. Pearson

The Whole by Contemplation of a Single Bone

Daneen Wardrop

Cyclorama

Terrence Chiusano

On Generation & Corruption

Sara Michas-Martin

Gray Matter

Peter Streckfus

Errings

Amy Sara Carroll

Fannie + Freddie: The Sentimentality of Post–9/11 Pornography

Nicolas Hundley

The Revolver in the Hive

Julie Choffel

The Hello Delay

Michelle Naka Pierce

Continuous Frieze Bordering Red

Leslie C. Chang

Things That No Longer Delight Me

Amy Catanzano

Multiversal

Darcie Dennigan

Corinna A-Maying the Apocalypse

Karin Gottshall

Crocus

Jean Gallagher

This Minute

Lee Robinson

Hearsay

Janet Kaplan

The Glazier's Country

Robert Thomas

Door to Door

Julie Sheehan

Thaw

Jennifer Clarvoe

Invisible Tender